How to Get Started

Bu

First published 2010

Revised 2012

www.hlsbs.com

ISBN-13: 978-1470164096

ISBN-10: 1470164094

Copyright © Helen Stothard

The moral right of Helen Stothard to be identified as the author of this work has been asserted by her in accordance with the Copyright, Designs and Patents Act 1988.
All rights reserved. No part of this publication may be reproduced, stored or transmitted in any form, or by any means, electronic, mechanical or photocopying, recording or otherwise, without express written permission of the author.
This information is provided in good faith for general guidance. It does not constitute advice. No liability can be accepted for loss incurred how so ever caused as a result of information contained in this book.

Contents

Introduction 5

How do I sign up? 7

    User name 7

    Welcome to Twitter 9

    Categories 10

    Find people you know on Twitter 11

Your Home page 15

Write your first Tweet 17

Set up your Profile 19

Set up your Mobile 22

Twitter notifications 24

Twitter Design 25

Followers 28

Direct Messages 31

Tweets, Re-tweets, RT? 33

Replying on Twitter 36

#Tags and Trending Topics 38

Posting a photo on Twitter 39

How to Get Started on Twitter and Generate Business

Twitter Etiquette 41

Using Twitter 42

    Tweet about You 42

    Tweet for others 43

    Introductions 46

    Tweet about your business 46

I want thousands of followers 48

    Who should you follow? 49

    How do I decide who to follow? 49

What is #FF or Follow Friday? 51

Twitter.com, Hootsuite, Tweetdeck ???? 53

Should I have multiple Twitter Accounts? 55

Should I let someone Tweet for me? 56

Summary 57

Helen Stothard's Biography 58

Contact Information 59

Introduction

Okay, if you are reading this then you are probably in the same place I was when I first joined Twitter. You know you need to be on Twitter but you still don't "get it". Neither did I. I was a facebook gal, through and through, how on earth could I communicate in just 140 characters? I was used to a whole facebook status to play with, and couldn't see how it could work.

So, how am I qualified to write this book? I'm not really, I'm just a simple northern lass who found a way to make Twitter work for her, and it's that journey that I am going to share here with you. I'm not saying that this will work for everyone, but it has worked for me, and if nothing else, it will help take some of the mystery out of Twitter for you. I would however like to point out that in the space of just a few months I personally had six Clients who could all be attributed to Twitter and this number has grown considerably since then, I know of other contacts who have also had success with Twitter, so I am talking from direct experience here, I would say over 90% of my business can now be attributed back to Twitter.

Before we go any further though, I do feel I owe a huge debt of gratitude to Nikki Pilkington of http://www.nikkipilkington.com, it was talking to Nikki in a forum that convinced me I should give Twitter a go, and it was some training from Nikki that got me started on the way to the Twitter addict that I am these days.

I joined Twitter in April 2009, and didn't really do anything with it at all till I started following Nikki's training in October 2009. This coincided with me setting up my own Virtual Assistant business in the September. I knew that working as a Virtual Assistant it was vital for me to build relationships via social media, and so far I had really only concentrated my efforts on forums.

To give you an idea of how far I came in a very short time, in just 279 days I had amassed 1028 followers (after culling but more on that later) and had generated over 8000 tweets. Now at the time of revising the book I have over 3000 followers and have generated over 46,000 tweets, you could say I am a bit of a Twitter Addict!

So read on, some of the information may be too basic for some of you, you may already have been there and done that, but some of it may be new to you as well.

I hope that through this book you will learn to love Twitter as much as I do, and that it will help you grow not just your business but also your social network as well.

Helen Stothard

February 2012

How do I sign up?

Well the most important thing before we can begin your Twitter journey is to sign up! The Twitter home page can be found here: http://www.twitter.com

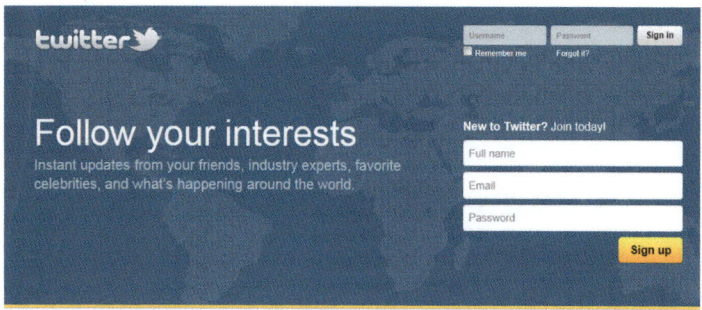

Click on the yellow "Sign up" button on the bottom right of the screen.

User name

But wait, before you start this sign up process take a moment, in fact take a decent length of time, to think of your Twitter name. It's important in more ways than one. One of the topics we will discuss later is re-tweets (RT's), this is where someone repeats what you have written. This is important in your use of Twitter; remember we only have 140 characters to play with. If your user name is 30 characters you make it much harder for your followers to do this for you. Do you really want to add _ and – to your user

How to Get Started on Twitter and Generate Business

name? You want to make it easy for people to find you. I chose @helenstothard, it's short, it's simple, it's easy to remember, it's easy to spell, and it means it's also easy to find me. So please, take your time, and get this important first step right. I tweet as @helenstothard as it was suggested to me that I should have a separate identity to my business. It's a personal choice but bear in mind what I have said about others being able to RT for you.

Got your user name? Then let's get you signed up...

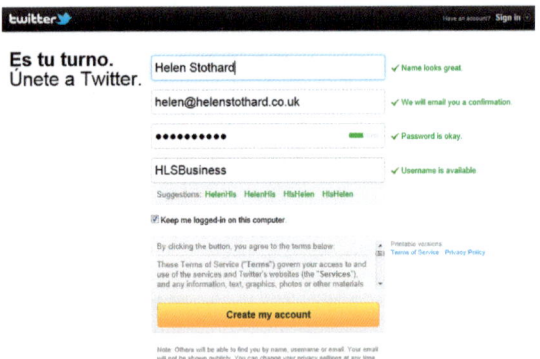

Twitter has started to pre-populate the sign up screen for you, and suggested a user name.

Full Name:

This is your real name and is one of the ways that people will search for you.

Email:

Your email address (you can only have one Twitter account per email address)

Password:

Enter your password in this box; it should be something easily remembered as several applications will ask you for your Twitter name and password.

User Name:

This is the name you will log in under and the name that will be displayed on Twitter feeds unless people are viewing under real names. Twitter will suggest a name for you, you can change this and Twitter will check that the user name is available once you've typed it. You are not allowed to use the word Twitter in your user name.

Once you have entered all the fields click on the "Create my account" button.

Twitter will now guide you through some start up screens.

Welcome to Twitter

Twitter has a built in tutor, known as the Twitter Teacher. Above you can see an example of a tweet. A tweet can have up to 140 characters, and contain links as long as they fit within the 140 character limit.

How to Get Started on Twitter and Generate Business

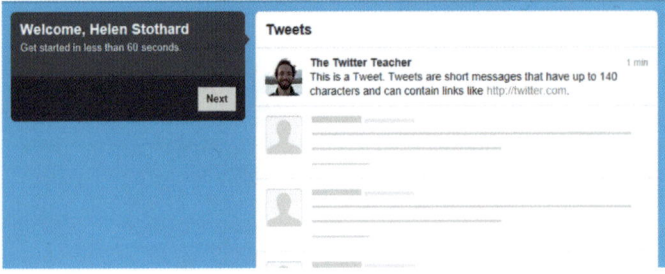

Categories

To help you get started Twitter will suggest some categories that you may find of interest.

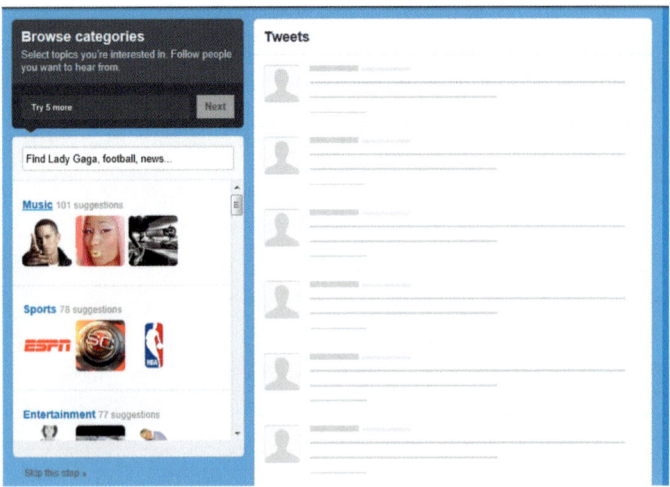

You can click on one of the images or category names to see further options. If you'd like to follow someone then click on the word 'follow' that appears at the side of their image when you select it. If you wish you can click on the grey 'Skip this step' text at the bottom left of the screen.

Find people you know on Twitter

If you want to look for your friends on Twitter then enter their name in the search box and hit enter. You could also use a topic word such as football or news. You will be given a list of suggestions based on the search criteria you entered. Just click the 'Follow' button if this is the right person. Use the 'Back' button to go back and select friends from your email account.

Click on the button for the email provider you hold an account with, (located on the left of the screen).

How to Get Started on Twitter and Generate Business

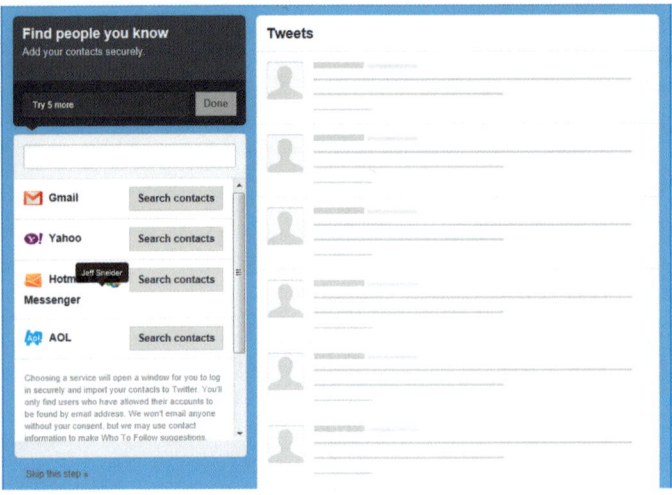

If you selected one of the mail providers it will now prompt you to enter your email address and email password in a pop up box. Enter them in the fields provided. If you select Gmail it will now prompt you to Grant Access.

Twitter will now contact your email provider and search for your contacts. Whilst it is doing this the symbol under the Contacting message will continue to move. Depending on how many contacts you have this could take a while.

How to Get Started on Twitter and Generate Business

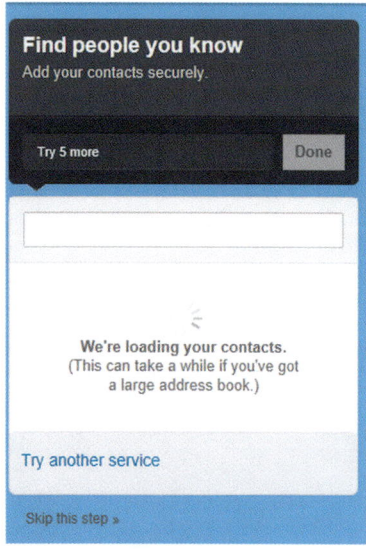

Twitter will check the people from within your contacts and see if it can match them up to anyone already signed up on Twitter. As you can see from the image below Twitter has found 567 of my contacts who are already on Twitter, I can follow them all in one go by pressing the button under the search bar. It also gives me a text link to invite the remaining contacts to join Twitter.

How to Get Started on Twitter and Generate Business

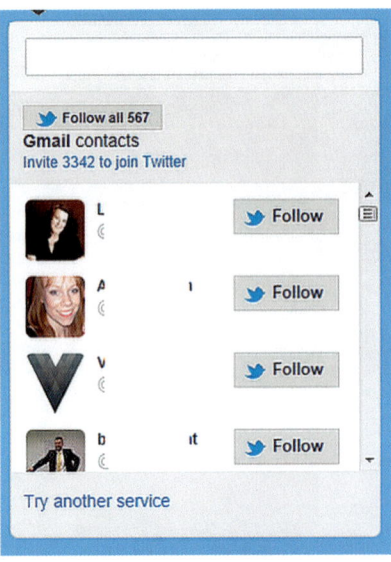

You can select contacts individually by clicking on 'Follow' button at the far right of each name. Click on the blue 'Finish' button. (The white spaces next to the photos are where your friends email address and Twitter name will be shown normally – these have been blocked out on this example). Click on done at the top of the page, or you can skip this screen by selecting the text in the bottom left of the screen.

In order to progress beyond this stage you will need to have confirmed your email address.

Your Home page

You are now on the Twitter home page. You can now see the most recent tweets from the people you are following.

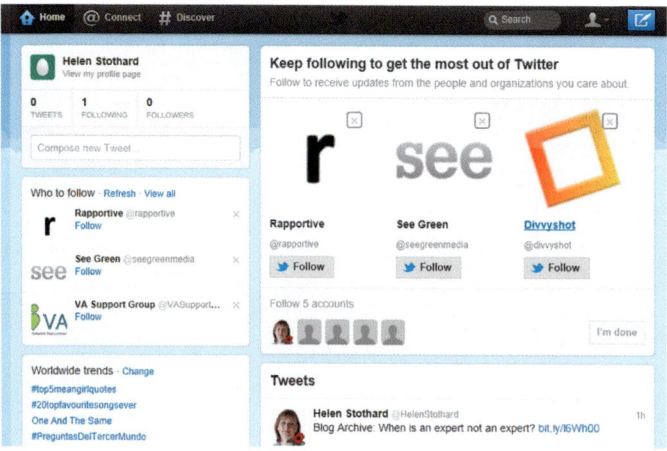

If you look at the example above we can see the tweets of the people we are following towards the bottom of the screen.

In the top right Twitter suggests more people for you to follow, it will do this until you have followed five account. This is also available in the left hand column as a permanent feature.

The top left of the screen shows you your information. You can have your own logo or photo on Twitter and this would show up next to your twitter name in the top left. We will show you how to do this shortly, for now you will be shown as an egg symbol if anyone looks at your Twitter profile.

You can see how many tweets you have written, how many people you are following, and how many people are following you.

Write your first Tweet

Let's click on 'Compose new Tweet' just under your profile information in the top left of the screen.

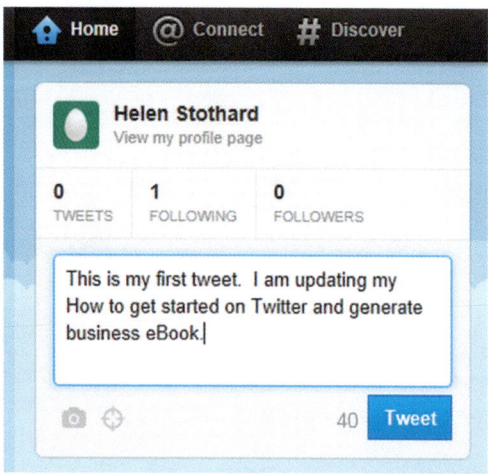

Don't get too hung up on the 140 characters, when you first start out it can take a bit of getting used to but you will be surprised just how much you can say in 140 characters!

If you look at the grey number to the left of the 'Tweet' button you can see that the numbers decrease as you type.

This number shows how many characters you have left in your tweet. If you don't have enough room just review what you have written and see if you can't actually say the same thing in fewer words. When you are happy with it click the blue 'Tweet' button but.....

Before you press the "Tweet" button just take a moment to check over what you have written. Remember, Twitter sends feeds to Google. Whatever you type in Twitter (other than a Direct Message) will be available to people on the internet. You may even have decided to link your twitter feed to your website.

Etiquette is that you use upper and lower case as you would normally. If you only use capitals this is classed as shouting, as it is in many forums.

If you are typing a web site address make sure to preface it with the http:// and not just start it with www. as this will mean that it will not be a clickable link. If people cannot click on the link to go direct to the site you are referring to you will find you have a much lower click through rate.

Double check your spelling, and don't use text speak. Once you have proofed your tweet you can click the blue 'Tweet' button.

You'll see a black message bar pop up at the top of the screen to confirm your message was sent.

How to Get Started on Twitter and Generate Business

Set up your Profile

Now you have written your first tweet lets set up your profile.

Click on the + Photo image in the top left of the screen. This opens up your profile screen.

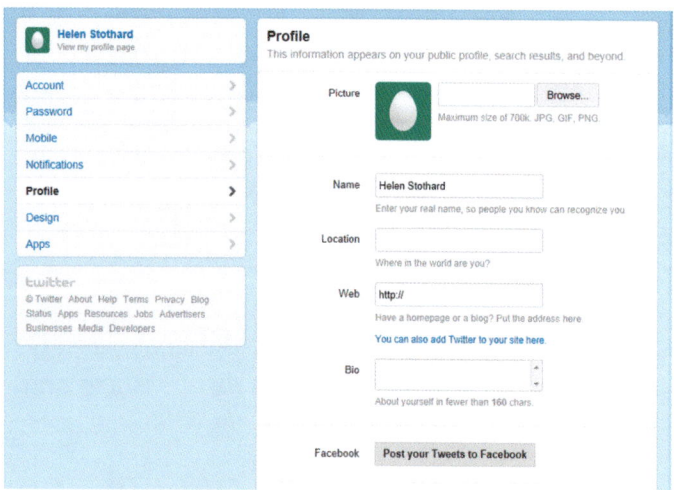

Your default image is a white egg on a coloured background. Let's add your own image so the people who follow you can identify your tweets easily in their timeline. Click on 'browse' to the right of the egg image. Select the file from your hard drive (remember it needs to be under 700k in size) then complete the rest of the fields on the screen.

Name
This is the 'real name' that you want other people to see.

Location
Enter your location, the town where you are. This helps people find others on Twitter who are specific to a certain area.

Web
This is where you should enter your website address. Remember the http:// needs to stay at the beginning.

Bio
This 160 character bio is really important. This is your only chance sometimes to let people know if you are worth following. Be humorous if you want, be serious if you want but do put as much info here as you can to help someone decide if they want to follow you in the first place. My business bio on my main Twitter account reads:

> *"Executive Business Support and PA services. Specialising in Xero, CapsuleCRM, MailChimp, Wordpress, Kindle publishing and assisting with social media"*

How to Get Started on Twitter and Generate Business

As you can see it tells you what I do. Some people have humorous bios, some people have work bios, some have a mixture. Make the most of this space as it could help someone decide if they would like to follow you.

Facebook
You can link your tweets so that they appear on your Facebook timeline, however, I wouldn't suggest that you do this, generate unique content for each of your Social Media sites rather than posting the same phrase everywhere. What is relevant to your Twitter audience may not be relevant to your Facebook audience and vice versa.

When you have completed this screen then press the 'save' button at the bottom of the screen.

How to Get Started on Twitter and Generate Business

Set up your Mobile

View your profile page and click on the word 'mobile' in the menu on the left hand side.

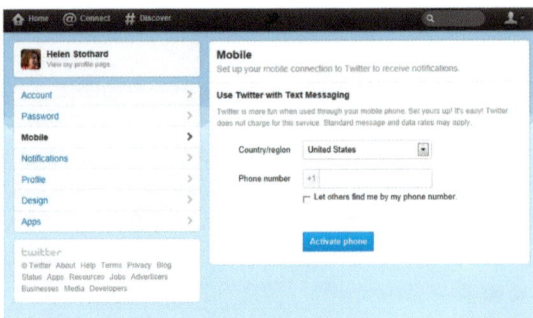

Choose your country, mobile network provider and enter your mobile phone then click on 'Activate Phone' blue button.

You will now be taken to a screen where you can verify your mobile. Twitter will ask you to send a text message from the phone number you just entered, to a specific text number. Shortly after sending this message you will receive a text message back from Twitter advising that your phone is now verified, it confirms the text number you should use when sending text messages to Twitter and advises that standard message charges apply.

The mobile screen will now change to show your phone. (Please note that you can only have your mobile phone linked to one Twitter account).

You can switch device updates on and off from the mobile screen now, enter an optional pin number, and even set a sleep time so that updates do not come through at certain hours.

If you add your mobile phone you can send tweets from the text message function on your phone, and you can also receive texts when you receive a DM or from users you wish to be notified of updates on. The instructions on how to use Twitter with your mobile phone are shown down the right hand side of this screen and are available any time you click on the mobile tab in your settings.

Twitter notifications

You can set these via the notifications option in the menu under your profile.

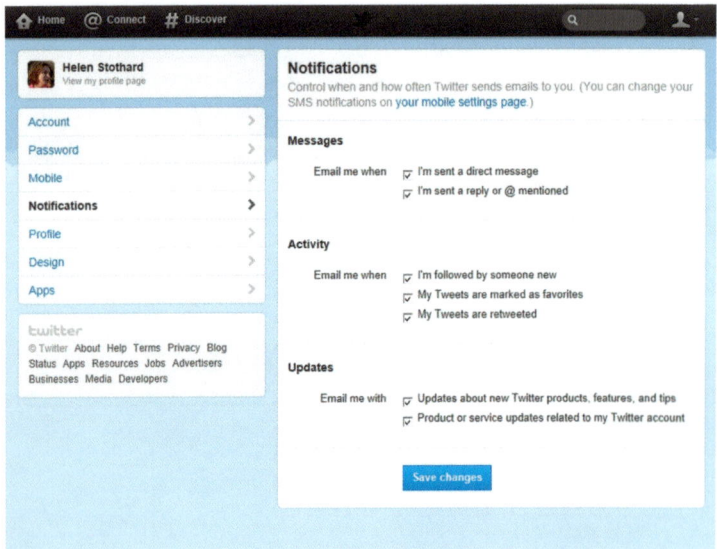

This screen is where you decide which notifications you would like Twitter to email you. It is up to you which messages you receive, remember your SMS notifications were controlled via the Mobile option in the menu. Click on the blue 'Save changes' button when you are done.

Twitter Design

This screen is where you control the theme for Twitter, or your Twitter background. You select the 'Design' option from the menu on the left of your screen when you are in profile view.

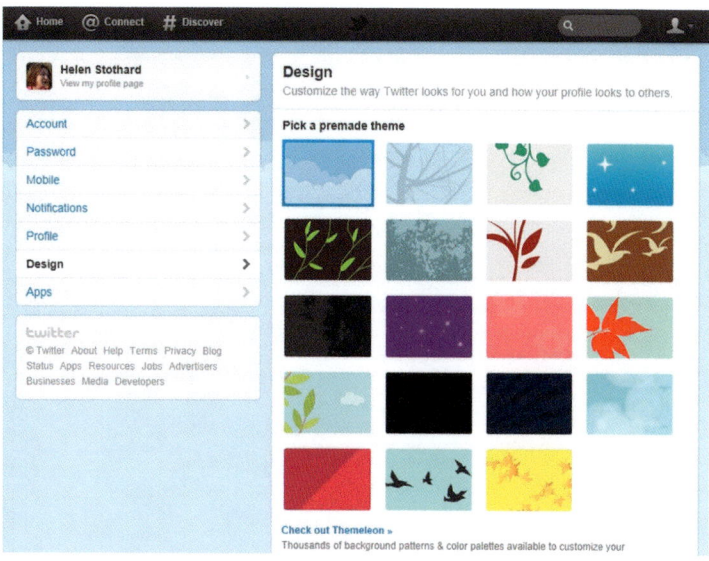

You can either click on the pre-loaded design that you would like to appear on your profile, or you can upload your own image. In order to get the best results from Twitter it is probably best to have your own background designed. There are companies that can do this for you. It looks more professional, and it's another way of showing your brand identity. However, Twitter have drastically reduced the amount of space available for your design and this needs to be taken into account when designing your own background.

How to Get Started on Twitter and Generate Business

If you wish to upload your own image you need to be aware of the dimensions you can work with. Also remember that your background will not scroll, just the information from the twitter feed shown in the centre of the screen, so don't show information that won't fit on this screen as no one will be able to see it!

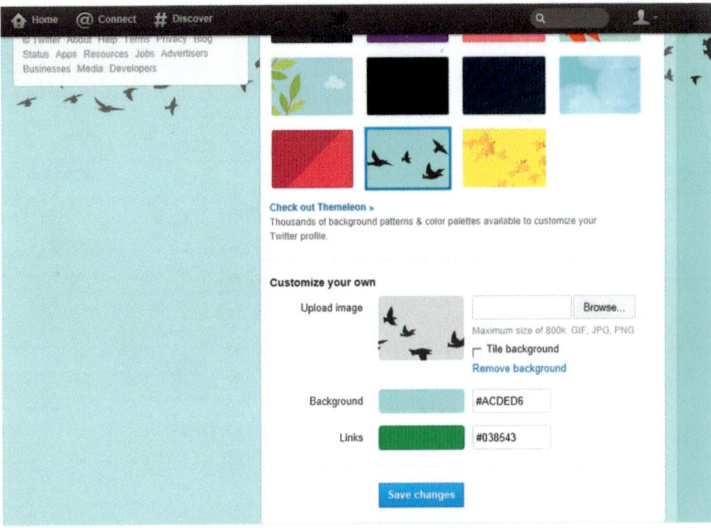

When you click on the premade theme image you also have the option of changing the theme colours. Just click on the colour block to select a colour or type in the relevant #code in the box provided. You can upload your own image by clicking on browse which allows you to select a file from your computer. When you are happy with the theme you have selected or uploaded click on the blue 'Save changes' button for the change to take effect.

How to Get Started on Twitter and Generate Business

Now click on the Home button at the top of the screen.

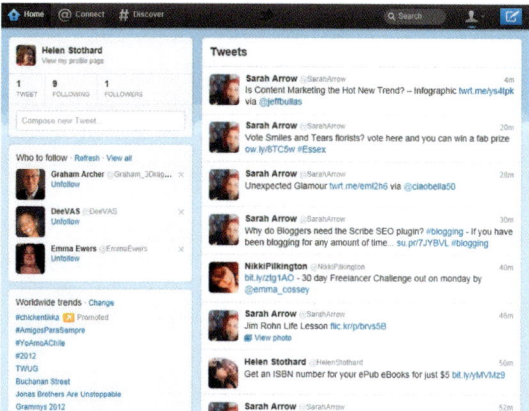

This is your standard Twitter home view. Just below your photo in the top left you can see your tweet count. As you can see we have so far only made one tweet. Next to this you can see how many people you are following and to the right of this how many people are following you.

How to Get Started on Twitter and Generate Business

Followers

Let's click on followers at the top left of the home screen again so you can see who is following you.

In order to show you how this works we have followed from our other account. Normally, when you get a new follower you will receive an email notification from Twitter. An example of this is shown below.

How to Get Started on Twitter and Generate Business

You are given the followers real name and their Twitter identity.

You will see their Twitter icon or photo, and at the side of this you can see how many followers they have, how many tweets they have posted, and how many people are already following them.

At the side of the photo you can now see the followers profile (remember that 160 character description we typed earlier)

If you clicked on the user name in the email it will take you to the users Twitter profile, or you can click on the 'View Profile' button in the email.

You can also view their profile from your followers screen. Just click on their twitter name.

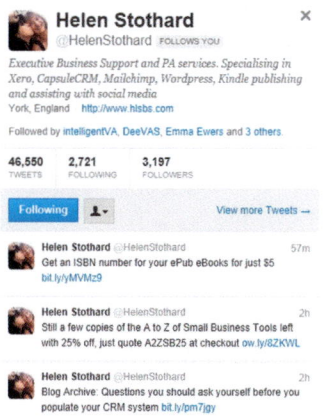

Their profile opens up as a pop up screen. You can see their real name, their profile image, their location,

How to Get Started on Twitter and Generate Business

profile description and the link to their website. You can also see some of the people who follow them.

We then see the number of tweets, people they follow, number of followers they have and their recent tweets..

You can un-follow them if you want by clicking on the blue 'Following' button. If you click on the head/shoulders icon you bring up a new menu of options.

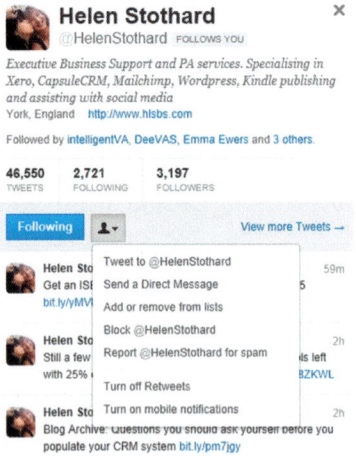

You can tweet them (send a message everyone can see), send a Direct Message (this is private and no one other than you and the recipient can see it). Add or remove them from your lists, block them or report them for spam. Sadly you will find spammers on Twitter, just post a tweet with the wrong word in it and you will be bombarded with messages from spammers. Don't worry, just block report them or block them and you will not see them again.

Direct Messages

To view your direct messages click on the head/shoulders icon in the very top right of the screen and access the drop down menu

A direct message is like a private message. If you send someone a Direct Message (also known as a DM) it can only be seen by the person you send it to, and is a private exchange between the two of you. However, take care to ensure that the message is a Direct Message as it is very easy in Twitter to broadcast to the world without meaning to. You can only send a Direct Message to someone if they are following you, and someone can only send you a Direct Message if you are following them.

The same rules apply as for a normal tweet, you have 140 characters and the remaining number of characters is shown to the left of the send button.

You will receive an email notification that you have received a direct message. If you have set up the option on your mobile phone you should also receive a text message notification.

If you click on messages in the menu at the top of the screen you can now view your message box.

How to Get Started on Twitter and Generate Business

Click on the grey arrow at the right of the message to access the message and be able to reply.

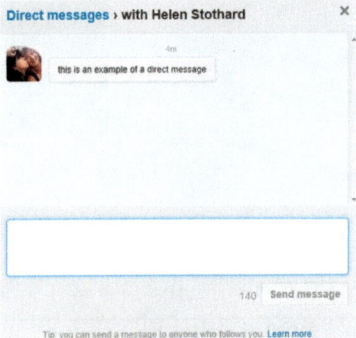

You can now send that person a new direct message by typing in the text box at the bottom of the screen. As soon as you start to type it turns into a normal tweet box. The conversation will appear in the box as messages are exchanged.

How to Get Started on Twitter and Generate Business

Tweets, Re-tweets, RT?

So how do you tweet? What should you tweet? We will cover the content of tweets later in more detail but here is a basic guide.

You only have 140 characters when you tweet. It's amazing how much you can fit in there. Let's start off with a short tweet to introduce you. Let's look at the tweets I have made above on my @helenstothard account for an example of some different styles of tweet.

As you can see my tweets begin with my real name followed by my user name so the other users on Twitter know who has posted the message. The first tweet contains a link to an external site and is highlighted in blue. You may notice sometimes that these do not show a full website address. This is known as a shortened url. As you can imagine some website addresses would take your tweet over the 140 characters allowed so there are services such as Tiny URL, Bit.ly or Hootlet which allow you to shrink a website address to fit. http://tinyurl.com/ is one of the websites that allows this. You can also save this

How to Get Started on Twitter and Generate Business

URL to your toolbar in your web browser, so that you can tweet a link directly from any web page.

The first tweet isn't by me, it's by Harrogate Theatre but if you look at the bottom of the message you can see that it was 'Re-tweeted by Helen Stothard'. This means that I shared someone else's tweet with my followers. This is the standard style of re-tweet and doesn't take up any of the tweets 140 character space.

The other option is a 'Quoted re-tweet'. An example of this is shown on the bottom tweet. Where space allows you can quote a re-tweet, and again if space allows add your own comment in as well. This is normally only available through third party Twitter clients and not via the Twitter website.

In order to re-tweet a tweet hover over it and look for the options to appear at the right of the tweeters name. Click on the Re-tweet option.

This opens up a pop up Re-tweet box. If there is space you can add in your own comment, remember though that you still only have 140 characters for the message.

Try not to shorten the message too much as Twitter users don't like 'text speak'. When you have done click on the blue 'Re-tweet' button.

Replying on Twitter

If you have seen a tweet that you would like to reply to hover over the tweet till the options light up as blue words to the right of the tweeters name. Click on the blue reply arrow.

Click on the blue 'reply' under the tweet. This will now open up a pop up reply box. It has put their twitter name in the box for you. Note that it is prefixed by the @ symbol. If you don't use the @ symbol they will not be able to see your message. At the bottom of the pop up is the original message that you are replying to.

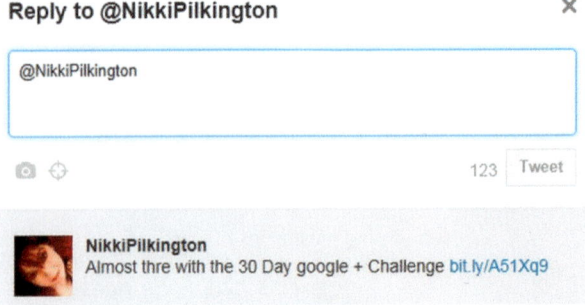

This is exactly the same as the first tweet that we made, think carefully what you type, keep an eye on the number of characters you have left, and remember that anyone can view this reply and that it will be available on Google when people are searching. Yes, that's right, Google is now using the feeds from Twitter in their search results. So, as with any forum post, if you would not want other people to see what you are typing don't do it. What is interesting is that when I did a Google search for my name the first result was a link to my Twitter account for all to see. My Facebook and LinkedIn profiles came below the Twitter one. This means that if you are using Twitter for your business you are getting into Google search results as well!

When you are happy with what you have written then you can click on the "Tweet" button and your message will now show on Twitter for all to see.

#Tags and Trending Topics

Twitter uses hash tags to create "Trending Topics". This is generated when a particular phrase is prefixed by a # symbol. You can see on the left of the screen several words and phrases in blue under the words Trends. This is where you can see what the most popular trending topics on Twitter are at the moment. You will notice that on a Saturday evening XFactor and SCD (Strictly come dancing) are very popular trending topics.

A trending topic is created when many people use the same #tag phrase. It takes an enormous amount of #tags for a trending topic to appear under Trending Topics. They can also be used to help you search for specific tweets when you are more familiar with Twitter.

Posting a photo on Twitter

You may wish to post a photo to Twitter to share with your followers. This is done by composing a new tweet. You can either do this from the 'compose new tweet' box under your profile image in the top left of the screen or you can click on the feather icon in the top right of the screen to the right of the head/shoulder icon.

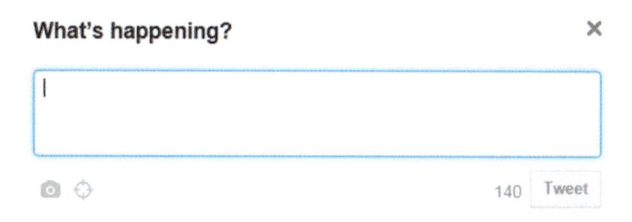

The compose tweet box is the same, you type your message in the box and the numbers count down, however, look at the bottom left of the box and you will see a grey camera icon. Click on this after you have entered your message but before you hit the 'Tweet' button.

This opens the file browser on your computer, select the image you wish to use.

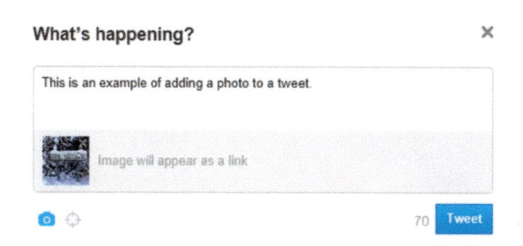

As you can see the image is now shown in your message box and you are advised that it will appear as a link to other users. When they click on the link the image will be visible to them.

Click the blue 'Tweet' button to post the photo for your followers. You should note that the photo tweets take a lot longer to process than a regular tweet so don't be surprised if you see the timer icon rotating for a while.

Twitter Etiquette

I will cover more about this in the next section of this book, but was asked for some tips on etiquette. Should you follow your followers? Should you auto DM your followers etc.

I don't follow everyone who follows me, I look at them and decide if they will be of value to me, sounds a bit clinical but some people follow me who only ever tweet about business and this isn't the type of person that I like to follow, it's a personal preference, I also don't like people who tweet about teeth whitening products etc.

I don't like auto DM's. I find them impersonal, it's much better to look at your new follower's tweets and profile and to send them a personal thank you. However, I would be the first to admit that I don't thank every individual follower, in the days when the numbers went up by one or two this was much easier than now when it can be ten or more in a day. Sometimes it's easier to send a tweet thanking all your new followers this week.

Using Twitter

So we know the theory behind Twitter. So how should you use it in practice?

This is the interesting bit. Everyone has to do the same in respect of using the Twitter website, the same way to post a message, reply to a message, or send a direct message. But the content of these posts and messages is entirely down to you.

So what should you tweet?

From experience and from the articles and reports that I have read, I choose to use the rule of thirds.

What is the rule of thirds?

Split your tweets into three distinct groups, and try and balance your tweets so that they are evenly spread out through these groups: you, the people you follow, and your business.

Tweet about You

The first group should be tweets about you. Not your business, you, the person, talk about the weather, what you are having for tea, how frustrating your child is, whatever you like, as long as it reflects you as a person.

People buy from people. How many times do we hear this? This is where you show your fellow tweeters just who you are.

But...

Yes there is always a but; you need to remember that whatever you tweet will still be seen by everyone, it will be available on Google. Be yourself but avoid swearing, commenting too vehemently, expressing political opinions that may not suit others, swearing or tweeting when drunk. You may laugh but you find examples of all of these on Twitter each day. Some people get away with it, others do not. Remember, whatever you Tweet on Google can appear in Google search results, this can be an additional marketing tool for you.

Twitter has so many different users that you will never please everyone all of the time, you need to find the balance that works for you. If someone particularly dislikes what you have to say then they can un-follow you, and if they criticise you, then feel free to offer this option in return. However, don't be drawn into an argument.

Tweet for others

The second group of tweets is probably one of the most important in terms of gaining followers, and building relationships. Tweet about other users, re-tweet for other users, thank them when they re-tweet for you, ask them how their day has been, comment on their tweets, engage them in conversation – you would be surprised just how much you can fit into those 140 characters!

Remember when interacting with other Twitter users that you need to use the @ symbol in front of their user name in order for them to see your tweet, and therefore be able to reply to you. If you type helenstothard I probably won't see it. If you type @helenstothard it will appear in my @ column and I will be able to respond.

Twitter is about building relationships, that is why it is called social networking. If you were in a "real" conversation you would ask the other person questions about them, their interests, and their skills and so on. This is no different.

What is important about interacting with these other users is that they have followers as well. So when you interact with a user, you are also interacting with their followers.

If someone posts a tweet that you think is of value to your own followers you would re-tweet it. What this means is that every one of your followers will see this message.

This is where Twitter really comes into its own.

John posts a tweet, John has 200 followers, and therefore 200 people have seen John's tweet.

I re-tweet for John, I have 1000 followers, and therefore 1200 people have now seen John's tweet.

Now imagine if some of my followers re-tweet for John, this happens every day, my 1000 followers have followers, John's 200 followers have followers, imagine how many people have now seen John's message.

We have helped John, and when we need a message to be re-tweeted John is more likely to do this for us now.

But it doesn't end there. When John does re-tweet for us we will see it in our @ column. We could just leave it there, but that seems a little ungrateful.

Send John a tweet or a direct message thanking him, but while you are typing that out make use of the 140 characters, ask him how his day has been, or if you have seen something in his recent tweets refer back to that. Show interest in John.

On paper this sounds very clinical and calculated, in practice it isn't. By interacting with your followers and the people that you follow, you will soon establish friendships and relationships. After a while, this type of tweet becomes so natural you don't realise you are doing it. How do you think I got to 8000 tweets! It was by engaging in conversation with my fellow twitter buddies and RT'ing for them.

Using the RT function can really help people. I have asked for information from the Twitterverse in the past and I have had the answers that I needed because my followers were kind enough to RT for me and their followers answered the question. This can work for you. This works both ways; someone may be asking for help with a question or just promoting some information. It could be that one of your followers is the one that can answer it.

If you read a blog or article that is of interest to you, could it also be of interest to your followers, chances are that it will be, so RT this. I remember one of my followers telling me that they thought I followed some really interesting people, I agree with them! By RT the tweets of people I find of interest my followers find new and interesting people to follow. I benefit; the people I follow and RT for benefit and my followers benefit. It's a win-win-win situation.

Introductions

Who do you follow? Do you follow people that would benefit from being introduced to each other? Have you ever thought about it? I know a lot of people I follow already follow each other, but don't assume it. If you see two people who should be talking to each other introduce them via a tweet or direct message i.e. Hello @xxxx I think you should follow @yyyy as you could maybe work together, or you could contact one and ask if they would be interested in being put in touch with the other person.

As you can see this second form of tweeting is not about you, it's about how you can add value to the people that follow you and the people that you follow.

Tweet about your business

Now you can tweet about what you are selling! You have introduced yourself as an individual, remember, people buy from people; you have earned the respect of your followers and the people that you follow, now you can tweet about your business or product.

You could tweet about nothing but your business, I know plenty of people who do, but then I don't follow them anymore. I don't want a constant sales pitch. I want to interact with people not machines.

Remember, Twitter is SOCIAL networking, not just business networking.

If you are in a room of people and all you do all day is talk about your business or product you will just bore people. Twitterverse is exactly the same.

As I have said before, whatever you tweet someone will probably not like it, but get the right balance of tweets and you will grow a loyal and large following.

I want thousands of followers

A lot of people have targets that they would like to reach in terms of followers. Twitter, despite what some people think, is not a numbers game. My own view is the number of followers is nowhere near as important as the quality of followers.

So what makes a good follower? Again, this is personal opinion but a good follower is someone who interacts with you, engages in conversation, and RT's for you.

Every so often I look at the people that follow me, as I have said, I don't always follow them back because their message or style of tweeting isn't something I wish to see in my twitter feed. The reason I keep an eye on who is following me is that I don't want anyone to look at my profile and think that I support some of the messages that are on there. There are some notorious spammers on Twitter, as with any popular social media. I either block these people, or in the case of the obscene spammers, I block them and report them to Twitter. When you block someone it means that they can no longer see your tweets and they will not appear on your list of followers.

Make it easy for people to find you to follow you, add your Twitter id to your email signature, business cards and profiles. Make sure you add links to your Twitter profile on your website (open in a new window so they can carry on browsing your site.)

Who should you follow?

Who you follow is entirely a personal decision. I choose who I follow for different reasons, and have a good mix. I follow some people because they make me laugh, I follow some because they are already friends, I follow some because they are in the same industry as me and I like to know what they are doing, I follow some because they educate me, what they tweet is going to teach me something that will benefit my business. I follow others because they write interesting blogs and articles.

How do I decide who to follow?

The first thing I do when I get a message from Twitter that someone is following me is to go to their Twitter profile. I look at their mini bio, that 140 character bio can give you a good insight into whether they will be someone you would like to follow back.

I look at their website if they have one, which can tell me so much more about who they are and what they do.

I also look at their last few tweets, is this someone who interacts with people, or is it just someone who tweets business every single tweet.

I look at the image they have chosen to put on Twitter, have they taken the time to share their photo or logo with me or are they still on the generic twitter icon. I prefer a photo as this makes them more of a person, but a business logo alone wouldn't stop me following them.

I also look at when they last tweeted. Does it look like they are regular contributors to Twitter or not?

Sometimes I can make a decision based purely on these elements, and will choose to follow or not then and there. Sometimes I just can't tell, so will follow them to see what happens. I can always un-follow them later if I find they aren't really my cup of tea.

What is #FF or Follow Friday?

This is a great way of finding new people to follow. Every Friday people recommend others that they think are worthy of being followed. The traditional way to do this is to use the #FF hash tag followed by a list of names. To me this doesn't tell me WHY I should follow them. I want to know more than that and don't really want to have to click on lots of different profiles to decide if I should follow them.

Another way of doing this is to use the #FF hash tag and just put one person in the tweet, followed by a reason for following them. This gives me a much better idea of why I should follow someone.

My personal preference is to post a Follow Friday blog link in my tweet instead. I can't take credit for this idea, I borrowed it from someone else, and who had also borrowed the idea from someone else. I have had great feedback from my Follow Friday blog. It takes a lot more time to produce, the links to the relevant twitter profiles alone are time consuming, but, it gives me a real space to write down why I think you should follow them. Whilst you can fit a surprising amount into 140 characters, you can't really sell someone in that tiny space as well as you can in a whole paragraph.

My Follow Friday blogs are my most popular blogs by far, and I have people ask me where they are if they are not there first thing on a Friday morning as they enjoy reading them.

If your blog is integrated into your website you have also driven traffic to your website that would not otherwise have arrived there. But that is a side effect and bonus of Follow Friday. Remember, Follow Friday is all about showcasing the people you are recommending, not about you.

If you choose to use this method for your Follow Friday recommendations it is a nice idea to send a DM to the people that you have mentioned, so that they know they have been recommended. Make sure you don't just post a link or they may mistake it for spam and ignore it, just add a couple of words to explain what the link is for.

Twitter.com, Hootsuite, Tweetdeck ????

How you actually generate your tweets is a personal preference. I tend to use Hootsuite on my laptop and netbook, and TweetBot on my iPhone and iPad. It doesn't mean that these are the best tools out there; just that they are the ones I have come across and prefer to use.

To help you decide what would be best for you ask for recommendations.

I like the multiple accounts and the way that Hootsuite will also link to my Facebook and LinkedIn accounts.

I like the fact that Hootsuite allows me to programme tweets in advance; this is particularly useful for posting the link to my Follow Friday blog so that it appears on Twitter before I actually get out of bed on a Friday morning! It will also be useful when I am working and want to repeat the link to a blog so that different people will see it. Remember; because Twitter is global, people access it at different times of the day.

Hootsuite also allows me to view the statistics related to tweets. If I post a tweet that links to my blog it will give me statistical information on how many people clicked on that particular link. These statistics help me to decide which of my tweets are of most interest, and to help me plan future blogs or posts.

I could spend pages and pages of this manual showing you how to use these Twitter tools, but they all have websites and forums that will help you with this.

Try a couple of different systems to see which works best for you.

Should I have multiple Twitter Accounts?

There is no reason why you shouldn't have different Twitter accounts, some people have one for personal and one for business, just remember what I said earlier about only ever tweeting business, if you have a business account do try and inject some of your personality in there. You can keep your personal account as somewhere you interact with friends and feel freer to express personal opinions.

Twitter does not want you to have multiple accounts, you can only view one at a time on the web version of Twitter, and you cannot sign up with the same email address for more than one account. If you wish to switch between accounts you have to log in and out.

If you do wish to use more than one account then you will need to use a Twitter client such as Hootsuite or Tweetdeck.

One thing to be careful of if you have multiple accounts is not to post the same message on all the accounts at the same time, you may have followers who follow all of your accounts.

A better way of handling this is to choose which account you wish to make the tweet from then to re-tweet from the other accounts.

Should I let someone Tweet for me?

Again, there is no reason why you couldn't employ someone to tweet on your behalf. A lot of Virtual Assistants, myself included, will offer this as a service and there are other companies out there that specialise in this for you. But, don't let that be the only Twitter presence that you have. I could research your business, tweet about it all day long, and set auto tweets on your behalf, but I am not you. I can't sell you as well as you can. If you do employ someone on your behalf then log on occasionally and twitter yourself, about your day, about your family, about the weather, inject that personal touch. It's this balance that makes Twitter such a great place to be.

By all means let someone help you with your twitter presence but retain your personal touch.

Summary

This book in no way covers everything there is to know about Twitter. This isn't a definitive guide by any definition. It's mostly my personal opinion based on what I have found works for me. I love Twitter though and just wanted to share my take on it with you. Let me know how you get on.

Come say hello to me on Twitter @helenstothard and let me know what you thought of this guide or feel free to ask me any questions you have on Twitter.

Helen Stothard's Biography

I have over twenty years experience of helping business efficiently organise and complete their administration. In 2009, I set up HLS Business Solutions to offer a virtual executive assistance service to coaches, trainers and consultants.

I am known for my pragmatic outlook and Yorkshire spirit – and am regularly in demand for ideas and inspiration on how to improve administrative processes and implement social media within the business marketing mix.

I am told I am an inspiration to many virtual assistants and people running a 5-9 business. I am one of the few people who have successfully made the jump from a 5-9 business to a 9-5 business. After only six months of running HLS Business Solutions, my proactive service and high standards were so much in demand, that HLS Business Solutions added in four team members – enabling HLS Business solutions to deliver a full virtual executive assistance service.

I am a straight talking northern lass, mother to one, a business owner, coffee drinker, cat food provider, good friend, enthusiastic but slow runner and a twitter addict, not necessarily in that order.

I recently celebrated the second anniversary of making the jump from corporate life to running my own business and I love it. Working from home allows me the time to be mum at the school gate and still get the buzz I need to be me (as well as pay the bills).

Should I repeat that I am a Twitter Addict!

Contact Information

Helen Stothard

HLS Business Solutions

76 Barley Rise

Strensall

York

YO32 5AA

Tel: 01904 890212

Email:

helen@hlsbs.co.uk

Web and Business Blogs:

http://www.hlsbs.com (HLS Business Solutions)

http://www.trainingforvas.com (intelligentVA)

Skype:

hstothard

Twitter:

http://www.twitter.com/helenstothard

LinkedIn:

http://uk.linkedin.com/in/helenstothard

Facebook:

http://www.facebook.com/hlsbusiness

Personal Blog:

http://www.helenstothard.com

Running Blog:

http://www.runfatgirlrun.co.uk

Printed in Great Britain
by Amazon.co.uk, Ltd.,
Marston Gate.